How I
Predicted
the Injury to
PRESIDENT
REAGAN

Sixteen Years Before the Event

KARL MEYER

iUniverse

HOW I PREDICTED THE INJURY TO PRESIDENT REAGAN SIXTEEN YEARS BEFORE THE EVENT

iUniverse books may be ordered through booksellers or by contacting:

iUniverse
1663 Liberty Drive
Bloomington, IN 47403
www.iuniverse.com
844-349-9409

Because of the dynamic nature of the Internet, any web addresses or links contained in this book may have changed since publication and may no longer be valid. The views expressed in this work are solely those of the author and do not necessarily reflect the views of the publisher, and the publisher hereby disclaims any responsibility for them.

Any people depicted in stock imagery provided by Getty Images are models, and such images are being used for illustrative purposes only.
Certain stock imagery © Getty Images.

ISBN: 978-1-6632-3261-8 (sc)
ISBN: 978-1-6632-3262-5 (e)

Library of Congress Control Number: 2022901840

Print information available on the last page.

iUniverse rev. date: 03/09/2022

#A visit from a Spirit; its mysterious message

Once, when I was five years old, I lay half asleep in my bed and became aware that there was a light floating at the foot of my bed. It said something.

I wasn't able to make out what it said, so I asked it, "What?"

The apparition repeated its instruction, but I was still unable to understand.

Now fully awake and sitting up, I again asked, "What did you say?"

This mysterious being repeated its communique' and then floated slowly through my open window until it disappeared among the lights of Chicago, leaving me to wonder what had been said.

I thought the creature could be a fairy.

Like the description of fairy's in fairy tales, it was tiny, and it had abilities similar to persons: speaking, moving about, acting mysterious.

And the term by which it was called, "fairy," was phonetically similar to another English term, "fiery," as in "the fiery furnace." The light that it emitted could be called, "fiery," so it had to be a fairy.

#*The problem faced, consequential to this visit from "the fairy"*

I felt special and blessed to have been the object of the fairy's visit, but I was afraid to tell my parents for fear the wouldn't believe me.

I also could not tell either of my two sisters, Nancy or Susan.

They were so naive and trusting. They would surely tell our parents about it and then my secret would be out.

Who could I trust to believe me?

#*A solution presents itself*

The following year we moved from Chicago, Illinois to Faribault, Minnesota.

I had entered the first grade, was making new friends and I chose to tell them.

Not one of them questioned my sincerity and to my knowledge, the story never got back to my parents.

#*Two coincidences; the first*

"What a coincidence," I suggested to my new friends, "first, I'm visited by a fairy, and the next thing you know, I'm living in a town called Fari-bo!"

#*Two coincidences; the second, part one*

Reverting to my earlier story, Chicago

There was one element to that magical interlude, i.e. my visit from the "fairy," that turned out to be significant, but which I didn't consider important at the time: It came on the heels of the first time my identity as a male was used to thwart my ambitions.

Back in Chicago, a subset of my kindergarten class used to be excused an hour before the rest of us were allowed to leave.

The half that left didn't miss anything special while they were gone.

I knew because I remained behind after they'd left.

I wondered if I was missing something special that they were involved in.

#*the challenge to explore: information acquisition*

One afternoon, I tried to blend in with them and leave, also.

Our teacher spotted me "straight away."

She called me out of the line and then informed me that those children were going to a dance class. Moreover, I was informed: I'd have to have my parents permission if I were to go along.

So I asked my parents.

Mom told me that I'd have to ask Dad. He was the breadwinner in the family. It was his money to either commit to the cause or no.

Dad was averse. He told me that dance class was "sissy stuff."

Naturally, I didn't want to involve myself in anything "sissy." That would have been offensive to both my parents AND myself.

I did, however, pine to know what kind of activity these children were taking part in: What was dance class like?

#*Two revelations made in that moment*

1.) I needed to see for myself in order to have a valid basis for opinion formation.

My dad's opinion was formed on the basis of his knowledge of other dancers and classes pertaining to them. He hadn't actually visited this one; therefore, his opinion was suspect.

2.) My identity as a man/boy in American culture hindered my ability to learn and explore as I desired.

#*Two coincidences; the second, part 2*

continuing description of my circumstances as they unfolded in Faribault

The problem of my masculine identity didn't go away easily, however.

In Faribault, when my dad asked me what I wanted to be when I grew up, I told him I wanted to be a rock star.

He asked me what instrument I wanted to play. I told him I just wanted to be the lead singer and not play an instrument.

He told me that only girls could do that.

The concord between what I was hearing from my teacher, Huberty, (and also what he was telling the other boys,)... and also from my father.

It was in March of 1965 that the mercenary nature of my teachers to the needs of the military/industrial complex guiding their activities became blindingly evident.

When he questioned us about what kind of job we envisioned that we would like when we grew up, all the boys were prone to answer, "pop star" or "rock star."

(The Beatles had come to America and were causing quite a sensation among our girls as evidenced by their appearances on the Sunday variety series, The Ed Sullivan Show. We watched him religiously.)

Some of us would answer, "movie star." The drawing power of the matinee idols for those of the female persuasion was also indisputable.

If any one of us gave either of those answers to Mr. Huberty's question, he would prompt us to give another answer by asking, "What kind of job could you see yourself doing until you get your 'big break?'"

> When Mr. Huberty asked **me** what I wanted to be when I grew up, my answer was, "rock star."
>
> When he tried to get me to name a less glorified and intermediate goal, by prompting, "What could you do to earn the money needed to become a rock star?"
> I answered, "I could be a movie star!"

I wondered, "What is it to him what kind of job/s we do? He isn't invested in the success or failure in our goals."

His only purpose seemed to be to divert our interest from our primary goals to secondary or even tertiary ones.

Even worse, he went on to suggest that it would be necessary for anyone interested in attaining the fame and fortune of our idols to graduate from high school with very high grades so as to gain admission to a college of preeminent reputation and thereat to spend the next four years majoring in a field of study other than either music or drama so as to enter the work force in a field other than one of your main interests and thereupon to spend an unknown amount of time as an employee of some company who would, by virtue of your lengthy training, find you worthy of sufficient pay to pursue your primary interest, which, as previously stated, was to attain stardom.

Right away, I could see that there were a couple of problems with his suggestion.

He was asking us to spend a very long period training to get work in a field other than as rock stars or movie stars.

No information was being offered about the processes by which groups or individuals gained success in the music or movie businesses, let alone an average amount of money required as investment by those attaining success in these businesses.

Nor did he have any information about what rate of pay any industries outside "the business," (as actors like to call it,) would or could offer you as a new employee that would be sufficient to meet the requirements of expenditure needed attain success as a showman.

He seemed to be a boob, a jiggling piece of meat entrancing us with the suggestion that it could help us reach our goals without having any strength of information or argument!

Underlying his contempt for my intellect was the far more damaging contempt for my basic right to liberty, the right to walk away from this fool and his many accomplices.

This was the kind of instruction that my parents and I had no choice but to accept under the terms of the terrorist Act known as Compulsory School Attendance.

And as an additional "slap in the face," my father foisted the identical suggestion on me, at home.

#Our government, source of terror for parents and children, alike

Mom told me that if I were to drop out of school, the police would put her and dad in jail.

That was the essence of Minnesota's compulsory school attendance act.

Not only that, but there was a penalty for me, as well: I could go to reform school.

Dad parroted the ridiculous suggestion of my teacher, Mr. Huberty.

Was the threat of jail so onerous that he was forced, by the state, to echo with me, at home, the absurdities I was confronted with at school?

#It seemed there was no escaping the abuse I was receiving at the hands of our government... at least until I turned sixteen. That's when the state of Minnesota allowed a child to leave school.

Dropping out at that age was also not an option for me.

If I, as a male, were not in school at the age of eighteen, I could be drafted and sent to Vietnam where scores of young men were dying weekly.

This was a rule under the federal Selective Service Act of 1964 for college "deferment."

The college deferment rule in the operation of this Act meant that, not only was it imprudent for me to ignore the insistence of both parents and teachers that I give my full attention to my studies, both at home, where I was required to continue with the work demanded of me at school, and at school, but that I, unlike my sisters, must give full attention to my high school studies so as to ensure my acceptance into college in order to avoid being "sent into harm's way," the Vietnam War being active.

It seemed the federal government was also involved in the conspiracy visited on me as I was informed by my father.

#I began to feel jealous of my sisters.

They were hugged and kissed by my father, "good night."

I received a handshake.

They could reward him with affection whenever he did something nice for them.

I wasn't allowed.

As girls, their teachers would countenance their ambitions to become artists.

As a boy, my teachers encouraged me to study math and science.

#Conclusion: I wanted to be a girl, too.

As a girl, people would love and respect me.

I wasn't and there was little I could do about it. At least for the time being.

#News arrives: a possible solution.

An army private had gone to Denmark as a man and returned as a woman: Christine Jorgensen.

On Sunday March 2, 1965, my parents and I were watching a televised panel discussion with and about transsexuals.

My parents vilified the panelists as horrible and indecent.

I remained silent.

#A new challenge: Again Secrecy

Afterwards, my mother came to me in the privacy of my room and asked me if I was homosexual.

I wasn't and I said so.

I did, however, note that she confused a question about my sexual orientation with the desire of the panelists to change gender, which she presumed to be born out of a homosexual orientation.

#Spy vs. Spy

The following day, after school, nobody was home when I got there and in a step out of the ordinary, the door was unlocked. I went in and it wasn't long before I was joined by my fourth grade classmate, David Swanson.

He told me that he was a homosexual.

What was I to believe? Should I believe that just when my parents suspected me of being gay, I was magically graced with the perfect confidante? Or should I believe that David was, like myself, confronted with the prospect of an early death just because he was male and needed to leave school in order to pursue his interests?

My goal was to strike an intermediate course. I didn't want to appear too friendly toward David; he might have falsely confessed. I didn't want to appear too distant from him; he might be in the same quandary that I was in.

By saying, "I feel the same way, too," I hoped to convey sympathy for him, without undermining his confidence by immediately revealing the profound and fundamental difference between us in our self-assessed orientation.

He asked me if I believed in astrology.

I told him that from what I'd seen of the monthly horoscopes in little scrolls that you could buy at Ben Franklin, downtown, that it was just ridiculous. Imagine basing your decisions on a forecast that ostensibly fits everyone born under a particular sign, millions of people, derived from some highly-involved superstition about what the position of the moon and planets during the month means for them.

Returning to the topic of our situation, I went on to discuss the ways society favored girls over boys, protecting them while using boys as cannon fodder in foreign adventures, acquiescing to their artistic notions in school while urging the boys to address the exigencies of the military/industrial complex, allowing them to indulge their feelings when hurt with tears while requiring the boys to put a lid on such emotions. Girls had the freedom to adopt either or both masculine and feminine trends in fashion, but not boys. Women and girls could be affectionate both with men and with each other. Girls were better loved and allowed more freedom of expression.

I denounced our parents and teachers as untrustworthy for the lie they were promoting to us, that it would be necessary to turn our immediate attention from developing as actors and musicians, accept their instruction with the goal of attaining a college degree in some other field, and then work in that field in order to earn enough money to pursue a career as an actor or musician. Theirs was a conspiracy to dominate us to our detriment.

What about life as a homosexual? Only ten percent of the population was estimated to be gay. Because of the deep hatred society held for gays, a hatred often expressed through anti-sodomy laws, queer-baiting, penalties and discrimination in all areas, he'd have to hide his orientation. How would he be able to find a partner in this small segment of the population when it was necessary for every one in this group to hide their interest in homosexual relations.

What kind of sexual relations could two men have with each other? It was my understanding that sodomy was their best option, but that had to be dirty and much inferior to standard heterosexual intercourse.

Then there was the option of changing your sex. If he could do that, he wouldn't have to hide his attraction to men. The pool of potential suiters would be the majority of men. His penis would become a vagina and with it, he'd have a clean and stimulating organ for sexual pleasure. As a girl, he could expect to be pursued by men. As is the custom, they would pay for their dates with, the now transformed, "girl."

I tried to imagine for him how they might make a vagina out of a penis. I speculated that they'd have to cut the penis off, peel the skin from the muscle in order to create a sack, make a slit where the penis had been and then sew the skin sack back in place, stuffing it through the slit.

I mentioned the TV program that was broadcast the night before: All men who had had gender re-assignment surgery or were being treated with hormones in anticipation of making the switch. None of them made for a convincing woman.

This was the problem: the age of consent to transgender

reassignment was eighteen, well beyond the age of puberty when a boy's voice dropped and he began to develop a beard. Society's prejudice against the rights of prepubescent boys made transsexual reassignment an ugly joke, allowing it to take place only after nature made transgender impersonation difficult if not impossible. Besides, who knew what importance female hormones could play in a developing genetically male body in the foundational terms of bone structure, as with other important aspects of physique?

My point was that if David were going to attempt a transgender transformation, it would be better if he did it now rather than later, but what could he do to gain access to the hormones and surgery he would need?

I told him about my father, (a surgeon), how he could never seriously discuss what he might do for David by way of making him into a girl unless he were compelled to understand that it was imperative for him to do so. There was a consensus that such a surgery is unnatural, a mutilation, a violation of his ethics and those from whom he required his license to practice medicine.

In order to overcome this resistance, he would have to take the first step himself, (a step I had often thought about when despairing my fate as his son, but couldn't bring myself to do owing to the extreme risk of an unacceptable final result and certain immediate agony:) David would have to cut off his own penis.

What would be the result of expressing his need for love in such a manner? Of placing his fate in unknown hands and circumstances? Of making an outward and visible sign of his alleged inward and spiritual state?

I quoted Jesus: "If thine eye offend thee, pluck it out." [1]

I suggested three possible outcomes: 1. the world was indeed full of magic, as per my experience in view of the existence of fairies, as earlier mentioned: His act of faith would be rewarded with a complete and magical transformation from male to female. (After all, we are made in the very image of God, He loves us and His powers are miraculous.) 2. the world held some magic: With the help of surgeons and drugs he would eventually be able to pass himself off as female, with a satisfactory vaginal apparatus. or 3. Utter disaster. A failure to adequately present a feminine physique would leave him rejected and scorned for the rest of his life.

The choice was up to him.

On the positive side, I averred, I knew that severed fingers could be reattached, which suggested the possibility that if, once he'd had the opportunity to discuss with my Dad, or someone else, what his options are, given his demonstrated seriousness of intent, he could change his mind about going through with the transformation and ask his surgeon to reattach his penis.

I explained why I wouldn't do it: I was too ugly.

I suggested that David was pretty enough to pass as a girl.

At this point in my analysis of the situation, I concluded that no one in his right mind could seriously consider what I was proposing as a solution for the problem as I saw it, the problem that I had illustrated in my argument, the problem of gender bias and its result, the desire to change sexual identity. Just as I considered every argument and piece of information, aforementioned, similarly

---

[1] Matthew 5:29 New Living Translation reveals the true meaning, but at the time I quoted this, I was blind.

tempting me to my destruction, as suggested, and had resisted the temptation, so David could never, ever, cut off his own cock.

As a playful and final inducement, I sweetened the argument: "By this act we are married," sounding the "a" in "married" with a short "a" rather than a long, implying that the act would result in a little marr-age rather than a marriage.

With that, David went home.

Thirty minutes later, I heard the wail of a siren. From my vantage point at the top of a hill, I could see an ambulance rushing up David's street in the direction of David's house. I called his number. It was busy. My father, a surgeon, came home and told me that he couldn't reattach a severed penis. David wasn't at school the next day and when I asked our teacher, Mr. Huberty, "Where's David Swanson?," he replied, "David, who?" as if he'd never existed.

I was angered. It was righteous. My father hadn't told me whether David had cut off his own penis. His response only suggested the possibility that he had. Huberty wasn't telling me the truth about David. His response indicated that he, too, was willing to create uncertainty in me. That's when I truly understood the hostile nature of the world around me. That's when I understood that by attending school I was serving the interests of those who required me to name a field other than music or drama when they asked me to tell them what I was going to do with my life. I was serving a government which held me hostage to a hostile curriculum vis-a-vis terroristic threats rather than treating me as a person with rights and responsibilities. I was a slave to those who held the keys to money and employment, denying me access to both on the basis of my age.

That's when I exercised the rights of a free man for the first time: "From now on," I said, "I will understand that whenever a teacher in this school system asks me what I want to do with my life, they are only asking me to name a field other than music or drama with the understanding that I will get a college degree in that field. I will operate in that convention until I graduate from college in this other field, but once I graduate, I will refuse to accept employment in the field of my training until I get a leading role in a major motion picture."

"Who do you think you are?" Mr. Huberty demanded.

"Karl Leonard Meyer," I stated.

With that I sat down and snarled at him with all the hatred of one who's been the target of an elaborate sting exposing his deepest vulnerabilities. I snarled until he said, "stop it." and then I quit... slowly.

Some time after that, my dad asked me if I'd like to go to another school, but simply changing schools would only complicate my life. A different school would just present the same problem, subjugation, in a different place. Furthermore, I would be unlikely to hear from my new classmates any news of David. I wasn't going to pursue that news, but I was willing to wait and see what turned up.

What if I were to find him at home, all safe and perfectly well? What would he say to me? Things like, "We really had you going, didn't we, faggot?" "Did you think I was going to marry you, homo?"

And what about the other possibility? Accusations like, "You made me do this to myself; you made me cut off my cock, you with your promises of marriage and the possibility of a magical result if I did! Well what are you going to do for me now?; it can't be reattached and I didn't transform into a girl!" What would his mother say to me!

The possibilities were too heinous to consider.

No, if anyone was going to have to uproot himself as a result of whatever was actually going on, severing ties with old friends and undertaking the process of developing new, it was going to be David and not me.

Still, there was something left undone.

Both my father and my teachers had established that they weren't interested in fostering my career goals. Neither he, nor they, had the authority to release me from school attendance so that I could address my goals with appropriate action. The difference between them was that my father and mother were targets of the state's terroristic threat, the Compulsory School Attendance Act. They were being coerced by the state and therefore could not be held accountable for parroting the misleading representations the state was forcing us to endure through our teachers, or the destruction of our productivity that enforced school attendance represents.

The assertion by Mr. Huberty that he and our other teachers were acting "in loco parentis," did not stand the test of reality when my mother cited the extortionate threat of the state as her underlying reason for requiring me to attend school, rather than maintaining that school attendance would best help me to achieve my professional goals.

Our teachers, by contrast, represented the will of the state for what it wished to represent to me and my classmates. I could not believe that my teacher, Mr. Huberty, had any personal stake in diverting me from my goals, and yet, he and previous teachers had engendered a special understanding about what they required when prompting us to name our career goals.

The federal government both allowed the abuse of our liberty by the state under the terms of Minnesota's Compulsory School Attendance Act in contravention to Article six of the Bill of Rights, "The right of the people to be secure in their persons, houses, papers, and effects, against unreasonable searches and seizures, shall not be violated...," and added its own language coercing school attendance by posing military conscription at the age of eighteen for males as a consequence of dropping out.

And what about the opposing point of view in this thing? Perhaps my father, Swanson and Huberty were only teasing me by creating the suggestion of evidence that David had acted on my suggestions, because they didn't believe that I was telling the truth when I said that I'd been visited by a fairy and, in consequence, that I believed in a supernatural element upon which we can rely. They needed to know that I had and that there is a reliable element of magic operating in this world. In order to defend my honor, I had to demonstrate that I was willing to trust in God by my conduct, just as I'd suggested to David that he could, in his.

Of course, there was a difference in what I believed to be possible and what I'd suggested to David. As one of three possible outcomes to "just cutting it off," I'd suggested a "magical transformation" rewarding his faith. I didn't have faith for that myself, but considered the suggestion to be a test of his ability to recognize and resist destructive and misleading suggestions, something that I needed from him if we were to be partners in resisting the forces that were arrayed against us, both in our families, at school and in the larger society.

Alternatively, if he had acceded to my suggestion, he had demonstrated the impetus that I, too, felt. He had told **our** truth.

What demonstration of faith could I make?

Fortunately, I was attending Jefferson Elementary. We had been taught about the Declaration of Independence signed by Thomas Jefferson, which said, "It is self-evident that we are endowed by Our Creator with an inalienable right to life, liberty and the pursuit of happiness." Was it self-evident? If it were, why would our government be so brazen as to interrupt our liberty and pursuit of happiness with a long stint of compulsory school attendance, especially the insidious way they were conducting themselves with my classmates and me? Didn't they know that that kind of abusive behavior was dangerous to them?

Fortunately, I had been paying attention in science and health. I knew that the average age women attained was seventy eight years. (Another advantage that women had over men, longevity.)

Fortunately, I had some logic. I knew that the longest period one could reasonably spend in preparation for a lifelong career was one third of one's expected lifetime, or twenty six years. A third of your life would be spent in prime productivity and the last third would be in decline.

Therefore, I reasoned that if, as a result of the government's fraudulent behavior toward me in regard to my education, I failed to make a professional debut as an actor or a singer by my twenty sixth year or the end of the first third of my expected life span, it would be evident that the government had caused me injury through its manipulations. And if it were evident that God endowed me with an inalienable right to liberty from the government's extortion, as well, then there should be a corresponding injury to the foremost representative of the government at that time. There should be an injury to the president of the United States at that time, in my twenty sixth year.

Accordingly, I sat down at the desk in my room and typed a letter to the president of the United States outlining the service I agreed to lend the government, (as solicited by the government's agents, my teachers, whom the government certified and whose curriculum it mandated.) I would attend school until I graduated from college with a degree in a field other than in music or drama and thereafter insist on payment before lending any more service in the field of my training.

I outlined the hypothesis of the experiment I would undertake in search of evidence that God endowed me with an inalienable right to liberty from attending such a school and the convention of speech which was engendered by their instructors, (the thing about my career goals.)

I signed it with a pseudonym: "Oliver", (as in "Oliver Twist" in the Dickens story by the same name; he asked for a second bowl of porridge, as I was going to ask for a second course of educational soup.)

Then I inked my right thumb and put its print in the "O" in "Oliver," which I'd created by circumscribing a fifty cent piece with my pen, and sent the whole thing addressed to "the President of the United States" with the underlying address the same as my grandparents' address. (I wanted to make sure that someone I knew had possession of this unique document upon which I was placing so much faith in defending my right to demand payment for twelve years of service delivered to the government.)

Accordingly, I don't know where my letter ended up, with my grandparents, the President of the United States or elsewhere.

I did, however, put the correct return address on my letter and one day, a week or so later, I noticed a man in a suit looking over our house. Could he have been a government agent, Secret Service perhaps, checking out a potential threat to the President? I didn't ask. I was awed by the forces arrayed against me and, for the time being, disguising my defiance of those forces.

I longed to record the events of this time in a diary. It seemed that I couldn't trust anyone around me and keeping a diary was one solution to the problem.

When I told my dad I wanted to keep one, he said, "Only girls keep diaries." Once again, my gender was an obstacle to my father's support of my desires. I didn't defy his suggestion, though; just as with my letter to the president outlining recent events and my response to them, a diary could be lost or stolen. Given the motive my parents would have to disguise their activities against me and refute my claims, I considered this a likely occurrence. I didn't for a minute think that I could keep a diary or its contents secure from prying eyes. My parents' domination and control over my life and possessions was near complete. (There was but one secret that I was able to keep to myself, one that I'd kept from David, too.) My father's resistance to my keeping a diary forced me, from the beginning, to rely completely on Our Creator to defend my claims.

It was then that I had the most amazing dream. I dreamt that I was with someone and he asked me whether he should pull a nail out of the body of this car with his fingers and set it, point up, behind the left rear tire, where it would puncture the tire when the driver next backed out of his parking spot.

I didn't know if he could do that and the simple way to find out was to authorize the proposed act, even if it set the stage for some delay and inconvenience for the owner of the car, so I said, "yes."

Then he asked if he should do the same thing on the other side.

Since my curiosity had been satisfied by the first act of knavery, and the additional inconvenience this second act would create for its victim would be much greater than the first, as a car only carries one spare, I rejected the option.

Then we found ourselves at a tree. We were carving our names into the trunk. I wanted to carve my name higher than his because I felt we were in competition with each other.

Then I heard a voice as powerful as a clap of thunder, "Now, will you tell the truth!"

I was jolted awake. It was terrifying. My heart was pounding.

Several years later, in seventh grade, all the classes from all the elementary schools around town were combined at Faribault Junior High School and David Swanson was again present in school. I never bothered to ask him where he'd been in the years since he first disappeared from class on March 4, 1965. I didn't pursue it before and I wasn't going to start up with that then. He was just some guy my parents had used to sound me out. He wasn't my friend anymore.

His reappearance, without apparent injury, didn't do anything to put me at ease in my environment. It was just more proof of how far my parents, teachers, and classmates would go to psych me out. Besides, honor still compelled me to my course. I still had to get into college and graduate with a degree I had no intention of using. Secrecy was useful to prevent my father from derailing my demonstration vis-a-vis the performance of my experiment. I knew that he wouldn't allow me to go through with it, if he knew my intentions.

Secrecy was also vital to my pursuit of another avenue of my interest: I wanted to know more about changing sex, how it was done, where I could find assistance, whether it was a viable option for me. I couldn't seek out that information while I was living at home, I would be disowned. By waiting until I was far away, in college, I would be able to explore this option privately, without offending my parents by revealing my interest. A decision could then be safely made whether to live out the rest of my life as a woman, if it seemed possible for me to successfully transition, or to reject that option, and continue life as a man.

The whole issue of what training to accept, what career to pursue, was secondary to the question of what gender to adopt. The opportunities were different for men and women.

To come more quickly to the point, I graduated from high school with honors and was admitted to Harvard, (where I finally confessed to a psychologist that, I felt more like a woman than a man.) While I was there, I searched the libraries of both the college and the medical school for information on transsexualism. I didn't find any.

I did find a paperback in a book store: The Transsexual Revolution.

Inside there were "before" and "after" pictures of one hapless victim. The "after" image was characterized as "an ordinary girl." I couldn't agree with that assessment of the result.

While at college, as an extra-curricular activity, I acted in many plays, especially those of the Gilbert and Sullivan Society. One fall semester, I performed in three plays and was so exhausted by the effort to keep up with my studies, as well, that I took the next semester off.

I continued to occupy the same room that semester, but without paying for room and board. I used a hotplate to cook food in my room and ate some meals at the Hasty Pudding Club. The administration didn't assign another student to take my room.

I also continued to attend classes and events of the college, but without being a registered student during that time. I learned that there was a tradition at Harvard of "ghost students" attending classes, but without gaining academic credit, a tradition born of respect for the pursuit of knowledge.

As a consequence of taking this semester off, I had a "March graduation." I didn't have a plan for what to do, next. One student let me stay in his room while he took a two-week government internship in Washington, DC.

My good friend, Karl Karandjeff, reported his college I.D. "lost" and obtained a duplicate so that I could use a copy to dine free at the various college "houses." The only "house" that I couldn't use it at was where Karl and I lived, Adams House. That was before Harvard changed to picture I.D.'s.

He and his roommate let me sleep on their couch every night for two weeks before getting fed up with the imposition and asking me to leave.

Word got around that I needed another place to stay and a

student who's identity I must conceal, "Q," offered to share his room.

At just that time, Karl's roommate was replaced by another student who was sympathetic to my plight. Without the pressure of the first roommate on Karl for my ouster, he had a change of heart and was willing to let me stay a while longer.

I chose to take advantage of Q's offer rather than to test Karl's patience any longer.

Q had an electric guitar and an unusual effects box, a "flanger." The box influenced his playing, which, in combination, produced a mesmerizing pattern that defied his ability to give it the structure of a typical tune. He also supported himself selling cannabis in various varieties, among other drugs.

One of the things he told me about operating outside the law was that doing so required one to be more honest in one's dealings than for those operating within the law.

His virtue did seem to be his salvation: Some local kids whom he sold to were caught by Boston police in possession of marijuana and rolled over on him. The Boston Police contacted the Harvard Police and my friend's room was raided. In a miracle of happenstance, he had sold the last of his supply just the night before, leaving no evidence to incriminate him.

On another occasion, a candle left burning on top of his entertainment center caused a fire which destroyed his stereo system. He was able to purchase a better one with the insurance settlement.

He was occasionally able to supply LSD and he offered to sell some to me at $5/hit. He cautioned me that acid was a very different drug than the pot that I had experience with. It was powerful and lead to new realizations about life and reality.

I was intrigued. I bought two hits.

On every previous occasion that my friend had sold acid, he had "dropped" with the friends he had sold to. On this occasion, however, he wanted to observe the effects of the drug on me, without being under its influence, himself.

The drug was in two tiny squares of paper, contained in a cellophane envelope. I took one out and put it in my mouth. In a short while, I experienced the usual effect of the drug: image retention in the retina. I could see "trails" as I moved my arm.

My friend had purchased many of his decorations while tripping, for how they were enhanced under the influence of acid. One picture, that he'd pointed out to me before dropping the acid, appeared to be just a field of flowers. While my perception was altered, (even enhanced, I might say,) by image retention, I could see images of lithe female dancers that were incorporated into the images of the flowers. Under normal viewing, those images were subliminal.

Since I was being scrutinized by my friend, I decided that it would be appropriate to do something unusual for him to consider as some aspect of how the acid affected me. He had a palmetto, a plant with hand-shaped leaves. I recalled the phrase, "bite the hand that feeds you," and decided there would be symbolism to the act if I were to bite off part of a leaf.

I did it, only to discover that the leaves were poisonous, producing a violent reaction in my mouth, throat, and stomach. I ran to the bathroom and spent half an hour heaving my guts into the toilet. The experience left me teary-eyed and weak for an hour more.

Throughout the course of the evening, my host smoked marijuana with me and we drank vodka, all to blunt the acute and heightened state of alertness that the LSD produced. The trip was beyond intense. No matter how much I smoked or drank, the usual relaxing effect of those drugs was utterly absent.

Six hours went by and there was no sign of the trip abating. I knew I needed sleep, but that was impossible. I feared the effects of the drug were permanent.

"God, what have I done to myself?," I thought.

Dawn came. It was a new day, time for me to leave my friend to his separate enterprise and strike out on my own.

I love early spring mornings just after sunrise and this was a particularly wonderful morning. The sun was shining. The birds were singing. Only a few people were up and moving through the streets and sidewalks with me. Gone, the mesmerizing visual "trails" I'd experienced when I was "peaking," yet colors remained unusually vibrant. The suspicion that I had permanently altered my physical state vanished like the morning fog.

I journeyed through the pastoral confines of Harvard Yard and was restored by its verdant beauty, pausing by the gate to Harvard Square.

There, grew a tree. A hundred names were carved into its bark. I began to examine the evidence of all the people who had memorialized their visit to this spot before me. Among those names I found my own, though I had never stopped at this spot during my years as a Harvard student. And a shoulder-width to the right, above that, the name, "Jesus Christ."

Eventually, I rented an apartment subsidized through an agreement between Harvard Student Housing Agency and a local landlord using the fake I.D. The landlord discovered the fraud when she contacted the agency to collect on the subsidy agreement and their records lead her to my co-conspirator.

Harvard graciously allowed me to continue to enjoy the subsidy it provides its students through the program.

By graduating with a degree in geology, I satisfied part of the requirement suggested my father, teachers and, by association, the government which placed them in authority over me, as necessary to earn enough money to pursue a career as an actor or musician. Thereafter, pointedly, took jobs in any field but geology while trying to put together a band with various friends and living at home with my parents, who weren't very happy to have me there even though they insisted I come home after college.

A few short years later, in March of 1981, John Hinkley, Jr. shot, without killing, President Ronald Reagan. The hypothesis to the experiment I'd written and entered in upon sixteen years before had been fulfilled. God does indeed endow us with an inalienable right to liberty, (a right being contravened everywhere by Compulsory School Attendance Acts,) in a self-evident manner.

Recognizing the nature and meaning of this event as an act of Divine Justice, it was incumbent upon me to inform the president in a way that would be as powerful as I could.

From my parents' home phone in Mankato, Minnesota, I called Western Union and dictated the contents of a telegram to be delivered to President Reagan at the White House. It read as follows: "Sixteen years later love's warning comes true. Bulletins ignored brought bullets to you. [A third line that I can no longer recall.] Convict truth's avenger, build a funeral bier."

I followed up with a letter of explanation for that cryptic poem... and waited, expecting that the government had a record of my original letter "to the president" predicting this momentous event, preserved from 1965, and that they would be able to confirm the truth of what I conveyed about it in this, my second letter "to the president." Unlike the first letter, which bore only a first-class stamp on the envelope, I sent this one by the most secure means available, Registered U.S. Mail, believing that my name would be cross-referenced to both my letter from 1965 and the recent telegram, that my claim for reward from the government under the terms of the contract between us that was implied, as previously described, would be recognized, and that John Hinkley's role as the instrument of God's justice would also be recognized and he would be absolved of criminal responsibility for his attack, even honored for his role in bringing a new-found liberty and newly-minted justice to the American scene, and released with appropriate reward.

There is one little blip in my adventure that I haven't mentioned: in 1981, after the president was shot, I traveled out to New York City to obtain a promised refund on a telephoto lens that I had returned to Olden Photography. While staying at the Hotel Chelsea, I met one Stanley Holler III of the British American Petroleum Corporation, which had offices in the city. He was staying at the hotel with a companion, Wendy Gross.

A woman who had heard me playing my guitar in my room and had taken the occasion to introduce herself to me, showing me her playing ability, was now my live-in companion. She was known by various aliases, including "Roberta."

I had had what I thought was my entire portfolio of stock certificates with me, approximately $10,000 worth when I left for New York; unknown to me was the fact that my father had withheld half of my stocks when I asked for them. I also had had all of my worldly possessions packed in my car. After several months of hotel living and travel with Roberta and two thefts from my car, I was down to my last thousand dollars and most of my prized possessions were gone.

I had discovered the Hotel Chelsea and its identity as a home to artists and musicians, by chance. This lead to my making it my base from which to explore an arts career, but with my money nearly gone, I was desperate to find a source of income sufficiently lucrative to support my continued efforts and strategy. Prostitution came to mind.

One night, after snorting Stanley's coke in his room with the two women, he said to me, "Why don't you cut your hair, wear a suit, and come to work for us at the B.A.P.; your father would be proud of you."

He suggested that we could attend rock concerts together.

I had been flying around the country attending Stones concerts, but my purpose in doing so wasn't merely an expression of being a fan of the Stones. It was my purpose to learn about the business of being a rock star. Before 1981, I had never attended one of the big arena rock shows. All I'd ever seen were local bands playing in bars.

I turned him down; I hadn't been working so diligently all these years to earn "enough money to pursue a career as an actor or musician" from and by working for the government which had solicited twelve years of my service, to cave in to their misleading suggestion, now, and let them profit from their abuse of my trust.

It wasn't long after that that I told Roberta that my money was nearly gone and I couldn't support her anymore, asking her to leave.

The next day, as evening was approaching, I encountered Wendy in the hotel's little bar. She asked where Roberta was and I told her about my circumstances, what I had planned for this contingency.

It turned out that Wendy, herself, had experienced similar cash emergencies and met them by providing sex. She said she could help me out and took me on a little trip to the upper East side where her Escort Service was located.

We walked down stairs from the street to a modestly-furnished apartment with a single phone and explained that we wanted to work. The owner of the establishment informed us that she hadn't hired out male escorts in ten years, but seeing that it was us two, she would make an exception and allow me to work, too.

I thought it was strange that she thought of us as a PAIR with whom she was familiar because I barely knew Wendy, but I was glad to have the opportunity to work, so I didn't dwell on it.

A call came in, which the owner answered: It was a man looking for a woman to date. The proprietor put Wendy on the line.

Wendy talked to the man for just a moment when she asked him if "a friend" could come along and join in.

The owner cautioned her not to pressure her customer to hire both of us.

Wendy persisted in trying to bring me along on her "date," an argument ensued between the two women, and as a result, the madam threw us both out.

I hadn't violated any of the rules of our employer, so it seemed unfair to me that I had to leave, as well. It also seemed strange that Wendy would be so adamant about bringing me along on her date that we would both lose the opportunity to earn any money that evening.

We returned to the hotel, and I parted company with Wendy to return to my room.

Later that night, a knock came at my door. There was Wendy with an enormous collection of her things in suitcases and plastic bags. Stanley had thrown her out, and she was asking if she could stay with me for the night.

Of course, I agreed and helped move her things into my room.

We talked for a while after that and she revealed her deep interest in and study of astrology, producing a book listing astrological "transits," or the exact times, by planet, when certain relationships are formed between the Earth, Sun and that planet.

This was a take on the study of astrology that I hadn't encountered before.

Afterwards, it was time for bed.

I watched as she undressed. She was oddly shaped for a woman, with broader shoulders and squarish hips. Her breasts had fallen. Unusual in someone so young. She seemed to be about my age.

I decided that I would sleep with her that night; after all, not everyone can be a perfect specimen. She had been my friend. Even though she was deformed, did she not need love, like everybody else? Would not the experience be just as satisfying, despite her imperfections?

We climbed into bed together and I began the usual course of my routine when making love to a woman... kissing... caressing. The one thing that I didn't do that I usually did was to perform cunnilingus. She had inserted some kind of spermicidal tablet and I didn't want to ingest any of that.

Then came the moment of coitus: Her "vagina" was cold and rough!

I immediately lost my erection.

Examining her nose, I could see a slight change in coloration that might indicate a rhinoplasty. Examining her hairline, it looked as if she'd had transplants to shape it.

Suddenly, the odd comment of the madam at the escort service made sense. I passed out with the realization that I had just "made it" with a transsexual and that that transsexual was my childhood friend, David Swanson.

The next morning, I was in a joyful mood. I turned on the radio to hear, "Hang Fire," by the Rolling Stones, with the lyrics, "Here's ten thousand dollars; go have some fun. Bet it all on one thousand to one. Hang fire."

It seemed that the world revolved around me because I had had ten thousand dollars to spend and had gone through it in a desperate bid to escape the plans that seemed to have been formed by the educational-governmental-industrial complex for my life and strike out with my own.

Furthermore, I now "knew" why David had disappeared in 1965 and nobody would talk to me about it: It wasn't because anybody was trying to psych me out; it was because David had taken his own penis off and everybody was so shocked by it.

I had so often thought about "just cutting it off" in response to my father's repeated suggestions that my goals and desires were appropriate for girls and not for boys that I was positively jubilant about having missed out on Wendy's fate.

Wendy, on the other hand, was in a foul mood. She was angry with me and didn't mind showing it. She turned down the radio.

I left the bathroom to turn it back up, again, and then returned.

Wendy turned it back down.

I turned it back up and told her to leave it at that level.

She defied me.

It occurred to me what dire straits I was in: We were staying in Room 100 of the Hotel Chelsea, where Sid Vicious had killed Nancy Spungee; my erstwhile friend, David Swanson, now going by "Wendy Gross" was angry, blaming me for a lifetime of misery and rejection as the result of her decision to become a transsexual, and now, she was attacking. She had known all along who I was, but I was surprised by her identity. It was an ambush, perhaps with deadly intent.

"Get out now!," I ordered.

"I have to pack my things," she replied while delaying in the task.

I was worried that she might have a weapon hidden in her possessions.

"You can get them, later," I said, "I'll leave them outside the door."

"I'm calling the manager," she reposted, reaching for the telephone.

"You can talk to him in person; he's just one flight down," I rejoined.

"NO," she replied, continuing to use the phone.

I grabbed her and tried to send her through the door with one hand, while holding it open with the other.

She slammed the door shut, nearly clipping my fingers.

I bashed her nose with my fist, stunning her sufficiently to push her out and close the door behind her.

Phew! I was safe!

I found no weapon in searching her things and dutifully put them outside the door when I was sure that she had gone.

I learned in a casual conversation with a stranger, a day or two later, that boys who cut off their penises are given a colon resection as a vaginal prosthesis, which explained why Wendy's "vagina" was so unpleasant. What are the odds that this information should come to me, just then, as mere coincidence?

I was arrested several days later, as I and a new companion, a man this time, were walking through the hotel lobby, exiting the hotel. I was charged with assault on the person of "Wendy Elise." She hadn't used that name when dealing with Stanley and/or myself, earlier.

I owe her my thanks for propelling me into a new relationship with the Lord.

Printed in the United States
by Baker & Taylor Publisher Services